Newhaven

in old picture postcards

by
Peter S. Bailey

Second edition

European Library - Zaltbommel/Netherlands MCMLXXXIV

About the author:

Peter Bailey came to Newhaven when he was eight years old in 1924 and will forever thank the harbour town for a happy period of growing up until he left in 1937 to join the Surrey Police. On his retirement he moved back to Newhaven in 1963. In 1969 he was a co-founder of the 'Newhaven Historical Society' and since it was opened in 1974, he has been Honorary Curator of the West Foreshore 'Local and Maritime' Museum, owned and operated by this society.

GB   ISBN 90 288 2745 5

European Library in Zaltbommel/Netherlands publishes among other things the following series:

IN OLD PICTURE POSTCARDS *is a series of books which sets out to show what a particular place looked like and what life was like in Victorian and Edwardian times. A book about virtually every town in the United Kingdom is to be published in this series. By the end of this year about 175 different volumes will have appeared. 1,250 books have already been published devoted to the Netherlands with the title* **In oude ansichten.** *In Germany, Austria and Switzerland 500, 60 and 15 books have been published as* **In alten Ansichten;** *in France by the name* **En cartes postales anciennes** *and in Belgium as* **En cartes postales anciennes** *and/or* **In oude prentkaarten** *150 respectively 400 volumes have been published.*

For further particulars about published or forthcoming books, apply to your bookseller or direct to the publisher.

This edition has been printed and bound by Grafisch Bedrijf De Steigerpoort in Zaltbommel/Netherlands.

INTRODUCTION

Rather than give a lengthy account of the History of Newhaven, I have attempted to incorporate much of it in the explanatory captions to the photographs, whereby certain facts and incidents can be readily associated to the present day scene.

Newhaven, like so many other coastal towns, had its defences on high ground from ancient times, with emphasis on the protection of the bay and the river estuary. At some time the river moved to Seaford and made an exit at the eastern end of the coastline. During the reign of Queen Elizabeth I this limb of the Cinque Port of Hastings, became choked and finally broke out in an area west of the 'Buckle', this was named the New Haven. The whole district was very marshy and many channels were formed and deserted, one of these later becoming the creek to Tidemills. This sluggish situation led to much flooding in the Ouse valley up to Lewes, the low land at times being unusable for grazing, even in the summer. This situation became so serious that the length south from the present swing bridge was straightened and cut to the sea, emerging under Castle Hill. This is believed to be the course of the Ouse in Roman times. The canal work eased the flooding upstream and a fixed harbour entrance was eventually established. The old Saxon name of 'Meeching' was dropped and the fishing village by the river bank became Newhaven.

The coming of the railway in 1847 was directly connected with the introduction of a steam packet service to Dieppe. The routes were extended over the years to include St. Malo, Honfleur and Caen. Also, there were regular cargo-passenger services to this harbour by steamers from St. Nazaire and the Clyde. The freights handled by all these vessels, added to the regular passenger and cargo sailings to and from Dieppe resulted in the 1880's with Newhaven becoming the sixth most important port in the United Kingdom in terms of revenue earned.

Three other milestones were to follow, the first was the New Cut made in 1863, when yet another canal was made, this time north from the area of the first swing bridge (yet to be built) later to become North Quay. As a result of this work Denton Island was formed. With the spoil from the New Cut, Pennants Eye, a backwater reaching almost to the town railway station, was filled in. These extensive alterations created an increased flushing effect by the faster moving water. The next major happening was in 1879 when the creek to Tidemills was closed allowing the building of East Quay and in this year began the dramatic Harbour Works which included the widening of the harbour mouth, the building of new east and west piers and the reclaiming of the area under the Fort Cliffs to create the promenade, this whole massive enterprise culminating in the construction of the remarkable breakwater and the establishing of a cross channel service free of tidal restrictions.

With the diverting of the railway track supplying the breakwater, to a new course around Sleepers Hole at the turn of the century, the causeway running from the lifeboat station to the Green Light was removed for a considerable length and with much dredging an area of this slob land was deepened to allow for a lay-by berth to accommodate two cross channel steamers abreast and moorings for two dredgers plus any yachts which could squeeze in. Destroyers were moored here during the First World War and a loading area for tank landing craft in the Second World War.

The deep mud to the south and north was not removed until the yacht marina development of the 1960's. Apart from the renewal of quays and piers (and a new swing bridge in the 1970's) there were few other changes in the port scene in the period covered by this book.

The growth of the town went hand in hand with the progress of the port. Industry was not encouraged, there were small concerns like the chalk quarry and the even smaller 'blue boulder' trade, when hand picked beach flints were collected and sent to Runcorn for use in glass and pottery glazing processes. The building of sailing ships of several hundred tons had taken place in the shipyards between the 'old river' and now Robinson Road, but after the heyday of John Gray the quest for steam driven iron craft, put the trade into decline by the mid-1800's. A small fishing industry has fortunately survived.

Newhaven town has been stripped of all its old properties and its few impressive houses have been demolished, leaving but the record of the one time existance of a Roman villa in the area of the present police station, and apart from the possible inclusion of the 'Bridge Inn' of 1623 there remains only the delightful old Parish Church of St. Michael as the sole re-minder that once a place called 'Meeching' was hereabouts.

Compiling this little book has brought me considerable pleasure, for at last it seems the sight of Newhaven how it was, will now be available to those seeking to find out. With this pleasure, there has also been sadness, for the need to restrict the number of photo's to the figure stipulated, has meant the rejection of so many lovely and instructive pictures. Acknowledgements will be brief, for so many of the photo's here presented, have come into my possession after passing through many hands, so that it is often difficult to know the origin or just whom to thank. I therefore extend my sincere appreciation to all those who have contributed with their pictures and information.

The view of Newhaven in about 1864, in a pale yellow and crumpled condition, was first loaned to me in the 1960's by a dear old friend, the late 'Ted' Arthur Davis. I am sure he would be very proud and pleased to think it had been published in a book concerned with the local Historical Society and their museum; the museum which he helped to staff when it first opened and where he spent so many happy and useful hours until his end. I must give acknowledgement too, to The National Army Museum, for permitting the use of the photo of the Armoured Train at Newhaven, and to my wife for suffering me during the preparation of this photographic record of Newhaven past.

Peter S. Bailey

1. The earliest known photograph of Newhaven dates from before 1864. A hedge bordered Fort Road leads down to the marshy area now the recreation ground. The first swing bridge has not yet been built. Denton Terrace with the Railway Hotel to the right, looks down on the backwater 'Pennants Eye' which reached almost to the railway crossing gates. This area had to be infilled with spoil from the 'New Cut' (later to be the North Quay) before the swing bridge could be built.

2. P.S. 'Lyons' (1856 to 1885) of 244 tons, she boasted 30 berths in the saloon, 20 in the first class ladies cabin, 12 in the fore cabin and 12 in the ladies second class cabin. The paddles were 15 feet in diameter. Navigation was from an exposed bridge between the paddle boxes. The 'Lyons' is on the gridiron to have her bottom cleaned and painted. She was sold for two thousand pounds. The creek to Tidemills has not yet been closed.

3. Looking across Sleepers Hole from the Fort approach in about 1910 the strange building, near, was known as the 'Ark' (or boat) House, it was in fact a semi detached wooden cottage, with slate roof built on an old barge, which had been brought here in the early 1800's from Rye. The bedrooms were in the hull with windows cut facing the south-east only. Positioned here on a spring tide, it became landlocked when the rail track was brought around the Hole reclaiming some land, by infill in the process. A delightful story entitled 'Carolines Kingdom' will probably be published in 1984 and is based on the fascinating diary of this intriguing lady who lived for many years in the 'Ark' House.

4. Bridge Street, before the First World War. The shops on the left offer postcards, tobacco and china. On the right hand of the street is the steam flour mill of Towner Bros., successors to the 'Tipper' Brewery, behind the hedge was 'Towners Lawn', here in fact the populace gathered for the 'Relief of Mafeking' procession. Between the lawn and the old river, was a coal yard. This whole site is now occupied by the Co-op grocery store and what is left of the one time R.N.V.R. Drill Hall. The shop in its front garden, was Hedges the greengrocers.

5. W.D. Stone's store – 'Shipping supplied'. Over the shop door are the words 'Stamp Office'. The lamp-post is at the corner of South Lane. The building behind was later to be replaced by a purpose built Barclays Bank, itself to be demolished only recently in favour of a site in the Newhaven Square precinct. The photo was probably taken in the 1880's.

6. Bannisters staff outing, believed before the First World War. The gathering is outside one of their High Street shops, the site now being occupied by Woolworths.

7. The High Street about 1910. The building left, was demolished in the 1980's, Barclays moving their bank into the new precinct to the left. 'The White Hart Hotel' was built in 1726 and was cut back in 1925 to allow road widening. Enterprising boys in the centre of the road, ensure a good cropping of garden produce!

8. A delightful study of the pace of life in the High Street probably before 1918. Mr. J. Funnel's horse is given a bucket of refreshment outside of the Southdown bakery, where humans could also partake of tea and coffee. To keep the gas bills down, it was quite usual for people to take their Sunday joints to the bakery to be roasted for a minimal charge.

9. 'The Blue Anchor' public house in the High Street, about 1900. Its site today is occupied by a furniture store. Reputed to have been the scene of many fights between local units of the Navy and Army, it was eventually closed down and became a greengrocers shop, thus ending the 'Beanfeast Parties' of by gone days!

10. A very early view down the High Street. Corbett's shop sold anything from a packet of seeds to a velvet framed photo view of the town. Corbett's was demolished at the end of the 1920's and a chemist and photographers built on the site. Next shop down is S. Noakes, grocer. A branch of a well-known chain of chemist stores occupies this site now. Below Noakes the grocer, we have Reeves the stationer, also sporting a Saving Bank. From the 1920's to the early 1930's this was Grangers the chemist and for many years it was left, locked and deserted — with its large glass jars of coloured water and endless boxes containing jars of 'Virol', occupying the window space. Such a mysterious situation led to the inevitable rumours of a bridegroom jilted at the altar and of the wedding breakfast spread, left untouched in the room above the shop.

11. Mr. R.W. Spinks is landlord of 'The White Hart Hotel' at the time this picture was taken, probably before 1914. Sefton Terrace, on Denton Island, can be seen at the bottom of the High Street.

12. Upper High Street about 1890, junction with Meeching Road. Well Court farm occupies the left hand side, the curved flint wall clearly indicates the frontage of the greengrocers shop at this position today. The barn on the right occupies the area of the present main post office. Webbers farm stretched from here to Cocksparrow, now transversed by the northern ring road. The townspeople went to this farm to buy their milk.

13. Top of the High Street about 1890. Well Court farm on the left and Webbers farm on the right, with a dirt track road leading to Brighton. This area is now a pedestrian precinct, the modern post office being situated where the trees are, beyond the barn on the right.

14. 'Vote for Beaumont the Liberal Candidate', ride a New Haven cycle! An interesting scene outside no. 37 High Street about 1910. Mr. French ran this shop until he opened a garage at Seaford.

15. Well Court farm and cottages occupied the area from the now Conservative Club to Meeching Road. This view looking south from Lewes Road is confusing. The cottages, left, were demolished when Meeching Avenue (now Southway) was cut through and the shops on that side of the upper High Street were built.

16. In the 1920's the Amy brothers moved their garage from Chapel Street to this grand location at the top of the High Street. Mr. Phil Amy stands with pride beside the Sharon Walker hire car. Under later ownership the garage was burnt down in the 1970's and is today the local 'Job Centre'.

17. Down Folly Hill, Lewes Road, about 1890. No Harpers Road or houses on the left. Turning right at the gas lamp on the Webbers farm building, the road dropped sharply down into Essex Place. Elphick Road had an outlet into the Lewes Road at this point until the construction of the northern ring road, when some of the houses at the southern end were demolished. Apart from filling in the 'drop' and considerable widening, the route is much the same today.

18. Folly Hill and the road to Lewes about 1912. How true is the photographic saying that 'part of the picture is often better than the whole'? This delightful study of children at play is lost in the distance of the original scene, which contained a much wider view.

The Convent, Newhaven.

19. Boarders and day school girls received an excellent education at this French Convent, built on the site of the 1591 'Meeching Place'. The chapel left, now the public library, has an entrance on the north side; the door seen here is no longer used.

20. A nun meditates in the Convent Chapel, this delightful building now houses the town's library, and could well have been denied the populace, but for the bombing of the Convent proper in the Second World War which prompted the order to move away.

French Convent. Newhaven
Farm & Laundry.

21. The Nuns Walk foreground remains as a footpath between Meeching Rise and Bay Vue. The farm-laundry building has been converted into houses, the chapel to the right is the public library. The meadow, sporting one cow, is now Neils Close.

22. St. Michael's, Newhaven's parish church, from the north. Southdown school now occupies the area of allotments. On the left is the memorial to the loss of H.M.S. 'Brazen' wrecked at Newhaven in January 1800 with the loss of 105 lives, there being but one survivor. The interior decor of the church is unusual being of restful shades in blue and terracotta. With its Norman apse it is thought to have been built on the lines of the French church at Yainville.

23. South Road about 1910. It is hard to realise that the children in this picture would go into the shop on the right to spend a farthing (one quarter of a penny) on sweets.

24. Christ Church, a noble brick building at the junction of South Road and Church Road. A hall, the church room, was added in the space to the right. When much of this area was demolished in the early 1970's to prepare for the southern ring road, urgent excavations were made to recover the numerous Roman relics, which have indicated the existance of a good class villa nearby. A modern police station now stands on the Christ Church site.

25. 'Michael Henry', the last of the rowing-sailing lifeboats at Newhaven. The picture was probably taken around 1900. Coxswain George Winter is the large man standing in the stern. He and his crew distinguished themselves with the rescue from the 'Peruvian' driven ashore at Seaford in 1899. In this picture, behind the coxswain, can be seen the old customs house at the fishmarket corner.

26. The Hull trawler 'Gamecock' having lost power, is driven ashore at the Newhaven east beach on 1st September 1908. This dramatic photo shows the crewmen up the foremast, awaiting rescue as one of their number is brought safely ashore by Breeches Buoy. To the right can be seen the lifeboat 'Michael Henry', being rowed valiantly to the scene.

27. The 'Gamecock' crew now safely ashore, the public give their attention to the unfortunate lifeboat, one of the first to be fitted with a motor, which has been driven onto the beach in the rescue attempt. A vagary of the petrol engine, when its services were most needed, it failed, the crew, less in number for rowing than would otherwise be, tried to carry on normally, but the boat fouled a groyne and was driven ashore. No loss of life!

28. The tide has receded and the 'Gamecock' is high and dry. Looking at the upturned half of her 'boat' at the stern, one wonders how the crew were ever expected to save themselves when in difficulty. 'Gamecock' was the leader of the trawler pack, fishing on the Dogger Bank, four years earlier, when the Russian Baltic fleet, at night, opened fire on them thinking the Japanese had come to challenge the might of the Tzar. One trawler was sunk, two men killed. An apology and compensation were accepted. One could speculate forever on what might have happened to the history of the world, if the apology and compensation had not been accepted!

29. 'Storm Harvest.' In distress off Littlehampton on 6th August 1912, the 'Anirac' of Genoa was blown past Shoreham. The local paddle steam tug 'Stella' managed to get a line aboard and with a tail wind brought its prize into Newhaven providing a scene of intense atmosphere. A sailing lifeboat, travelled with the two vessels.

30. A charming scene in the recreation ground in 1899. These spectators are in the area which was later used for the football ground. At the rear can be seen the stables for the horses at the chalk quarry. Newhaven acquired its recreation ground through the interest and goodwill of the Earl of Sheffield, whose cricket team played the 'Newhaveners' on this inaugural occasion.

31. A picture of considerable interest of about 1910. On the skyline left, is the parish church. The large house is 'Grays'. It is probable that the area between the bottom of the path and the first house of Gibbon Road is the location of the picture showing the threshing engine (picture 64). Trucks from Colegate and Gray's Quarry can be seen. In the recreation ground is a lake which resulted from the digging for clay to make the bricks to build the Fort in the 1860's. The kilns for baking the bricks were situated at the southern side of the recreation ground.

32. The old cobbled cottages in Chapel Street about 1913. These were opposite the 'Jolly Sailor' leading southwards. Two into one, extensively modernised and perhaps painted white, one can speculate on what a potential jewel was lost, when these fine examples of Sussex pebble craft, were demolished after the Second World War.

33. Meeching Road, northern end. A gracious pace of life about 1907. 'Saxonholme' left (earlier 'Dacre Villa') conveys an air of comfortable wealth. The far end of the flint wall where the group are talking has yet to make way for Marshall Lane to serve the rear of the new shops in upper High Street. Near from the lane has yet to be built the 'Kinema' later to become the town's fire station. The fine Georgian house is 'Sussex Lodge' at one time a boarding school for young gentleman. Like 'Saxonholme' it has also housed the town's doctors. To the right of the boy with the pram can just be seen the town's new general post office.

34. Boasting its date of building, top centre, of 1904, the new and first purpose built post office looks down on a delightful selection of the populace. Opposite is 'Saxonholme'. Meeching Road was nicknamed 'Piano Street' for in its earlier days it housed the 'posher' element of the town who were more likely to be able to afford pianos. At the far end of the road can be seen the roof top of Meeching Court farm. The Congregational Chapel corners with Meeching Rise, the Sunday school has filled in the gap between the chapel proper and the first house beyond in Meeching Road.

35. The 'Phoenix Arms' public house and butchers shop in Meeching Road, 1860. These were the two most northern houses on the west side. A Congregational Chapel was built to the right of the picture, although a gap was left between the two sites. This space was later filled with a Sunday school extension to the Chapel. The latter has not been used for worship for many years, the scene is still much the same in 1983, but the terraced houses are now purely residential.

36. A picture packed with interest, taken from Western Road about 1910. The boys school looks very smart with its bell tower. In the left foreground, between Bay View and the school, can be seen a white post, there are two more of these leading down to South Road, these were used to carry an electric cable from the 'Company's' supply at West Quay. The cable went to the harbour masters house 'Cathay' (later 'Dunalister') in Western Road and was therefore the first house in Newhaven to be lit by electricity.

37. Fort Road about 1906, looking north. The near house is of considerable interest. At the time of this picture it is advertised 'To Let', but in 1891 it was rented to a certain Charles Wells, who won fifty thousand pounds in one night at Monte Carlo. It was about this remarkable win that the song 'The man who broke the bank at Monte Carlo' was based. He had taken the house as his riotous parties at the 'London and Paris Hotel' had prompted the request for him to seek other accommodation. Wells shared the fate of most gamblers and died a pauper.

Old Piers, Newhaven. The Mill Series.

38. The old narrow harbour entrance about 1870. After 1879 the east pier was rebuilt making the entrance wider. The small lighthouse, right, was moved first to beside the lifeboat house and later to near the old swing bridge, where it became a shed, until it was taken to 'Tideway' school for restoration, where it still stands. The bridge left is over the water entrance to the wet moat. Under the bridge was later made solid, but retained a sluice for the sea water to flow.

39. Construction of the promenade wall in November 1879. The steps down which so many happy feet tread every summer to the sand beach, are just being built. This picture shows the slope of the cliffs and the white shirts of some of the navvies, to the right, starting another dig. The area between the wall and the shingle beach has not yet been filled with the cliff spoil.

40. From the sea wall around where is now the sand beach, contractors huts litter the area we see covered with grass. The space between the shingle and the wall was filled in with chalk and rubble from the cliffs to the west. The right hand section of the concrete wall on the Fort slipped down in the early 1960's. In the extreme right of the picture can be seen the lighthouse keeper's wooden residence. To the left of this is today the Local and Maritime Museum. The picture was taken in December 1879.

41. A scene in November 1881 shows the massive steam concrete mixer, situated towards the southern end of now East Quay, where the concrete was prepared for the foundations of the breakwater. Moored beneath the spout is the steam hopper 'Trident' specially built for the task. Into her hold would be positioned a large tarpaulin bag, into which 104 tons of concrete was poured. The bag was then laced over and the 'Trident' would steam out to the site of the foundations and would drop the bag through her opening bottom.

42. The breakwater under construction, low tide, August 1883. Foundations have been established by dropping bag on bag of 104 tons of concrete until a level above low tide water is achieved, then the upper works can be built using conventional wooden shuttering and concrete prepared by a steam mixer on the breakwater which can be seen to the left of the overhanging structure.

43. The part completed breakwater 1882-83, already an impressive piece of structure achieved with such limited equipment. The beach to the left is now all sand and that to the right, shingle, the 'Fricker' rocks have all disappeared from sight. For the building of the breakwater a new harbour company was formed in 1878, work started in 1879 and finished in 1893. The length is 2,700 feet, 175,000 tons of concrete were used and including new piers and the East Quay the cost was upwards of six hundred thousand pounds!

44. Umbrellas, as sun shades, indicate that the Newhaven Regatta of 7th August 1882 has struck lovely weather. Special trains were run from London, Brighton and Eastbourne. Two hundred pounds was spent on a firework display and three hundred in prizes; a lot of money in those days. The large paddle steamer is the 'Alexandra', a one time Newhaven-Dieppe packet, but here an excursion steamer operated by a Hastings company. Beyond the group of sailing craft can be seen the hopper 'Trident' which was 'committee boat' for the day.

45. The attractive west pier lighthouse about 1885. On the left is suspended the fog bell. Before radar, when the mail boats were seeking the harbour in dense fog, maroons would be fired to bring them within range of the foghorn at the breakwater end. Then later, the bell would be rung to indicate the harbour mouth. Owing to a foundations slip of the west pier in the 1970's, this lovely lighthouse became unsafe and was blown up.

46. The 'end product' after all the disturbance from 1879 onwards, culminating in a wider harbour entrance, new east and west piers, a promenade reclaimed from the sea, with cliff infill and a magnificent new breakwater. This impressive picture of about 1903, shows the S.S. 'Arundel' entering what must have been paradise for the masters of these fast but 'tender' steamers, compared with the harbour approaches of the earlier period. Shingle has since built up to the west of the breakwater, but in this picture the sea still laps the promenade at high water.

47. The wonderful swing bridge, opened to the public after noon on 22nd December 1866. Unlike the one it replaced, this was free to all users. It was turned by a removable capstan, with four poles each pushed by two men. The houses are Denton Terrace with the 'Railway Hotel' to the right. These disappeared with the construction of the railway fly over. In this picture, the 'New Cut' has been made, but the North Quay as such was not constructed until the latter part of the last century.

48. Some time soon after 1905, the Newhaven built and registered 'Sussex Maid', takes on chalk ballast from the quarry. Her last years were spent in bringing coal from the Tyne for the local 'Co-op'. Alongside her is Richard R. Collard's pleasure steamer 'Southampton'. This little paddler frequently took day trippers from Eastbourne and Hastings across to Blankenberg, near Ostend. The cargo steamer right, is the 'Dieppe Screw' 'Caen'.

49. Tall ships at West bank soon after 1900. The 'London and Paris' Hotel is on the left. At the adjoining Railway Quay is moored one of the services regular cargo steamers, known as the 'Dieppe Screws'. This expression came into usage by the local dock workers during the last century. It was a term to differentiate between the cargo carrying service, which had been propellor driven from the beginning, as opposed to the passenger steamers, which had been paddlers until the introduction of 'Seine' in 1890.

50. A smart body of men! Newhaven fire brigade with their horse drawn manual pump engine outside its station, one of the large doors of which is just visible on the left. In the background are the council offices and the space once occupied to house this appliance and an escape ladder on wheels, is now the Council Chamber.

51. An immaculate Mr. Bussey poses at the reins of his horse cab, so sadly associated with journeys to the cemetery. The building behind is now the Harbour garage with Clifton Terrace just showing. This picture was taken in the mid-1920's.

52. Messrs. H. Penfold (near) and W. Bussey, show off the latest in taxis, based in Railway Road in the mid-1920's. The open car is of course Henry Ford's famous model 'T', the 'Tin Lizzie' so favoured with the 'Keystone Cops' of the silent film era. Clifton Terrace is in the background and to the left Parkstone Villas can be seen, now no longer with us.

53. The little harbour works loco, 'Bishopstone', on the West Bank December 1879. She was super-
seded by the 'Fenchurch' which spent so much of her life at Newhaven and is still running on the
'Bluebell Railway'.

54. Britain's first armoured train on the east beach rail track. A brain child and product of the Brighton Loco Works, where many of the employees were also members of a volunteer coastal defence force, and their O.C. also a director of the railway company. The turret contained a 40 pound rapid breach loading field gun. The whole was traversed by four men pushing on two long poles inserted into the rear corners of the turret. It was first demonstrated at Newhaven, before notables in 1894. The 'Saddle' tank 'Bradford' and a sister engine, 'Wave', were used around the harbour.

55. The 'Bridge Hotel' (now once again the 'Bridge Inn'). This is where Louis Philippe, the last king of France, spent his first night in exile, with his queen in 1848. The royal party made their escape in the steamer 'Express' and were rowed from this vessel into the harbour, stepping ashore in the area of the present day lifeboat house. The toll house belonging to the old draw bridge can be seen at the left of the hotel.

Old Toll Bridge & Toll House, Newhaven.

56. The act to build Newhaven's first bridge was passed by George III in 1784. Previously the crossing was made by ferry from the bottom of the High Street. The two moving sections of the draw bridge were lifted by winches but the pivoted supports beneath created a backwards sliding movement as well, which facilitated the closing action by virtue of the weight and pivoting of each of the spans.

57. Washers Wharf at the turn of the century. The ring road, North Way, follows much the same course. The dredger left is the 'Hercules', built in 1842. Moving to the right through the gap can be seen the 'Co-op' stores, boasting two storeys. Next is the steam flour mill and to the right again is the Tipper brewery and moored outside is the paddle tug named after this famous brew. The dredger to the right with two funnels is the self propelled 'Neptune'.

58. As recently as the 1930's, a woman feeds a mixture of swans, geese and ducks from the West Bank of the old river. The 'Blacksmith's Arms' public house was on the right just out of the picture. The large building is Stricklands granary, which was destroyed by fire on 11th February 1940, but not from enemy action (left distance).

59. In the old river in the mid-1930's. To the left of the Island Bridge are Catts Cottages and to the right Sefton Terrace. The steam hopper moored at the stage is the 'Trident' which was built to lay the foundations of the breakwater. Here she is rusting away her last days, but surprisingly she occasionally did a turn of concrete block dropping at the breakwater and when a tug was out of action she could be seen towing mud barges.

Old Ship Yard, Newhaven.

60. This shipyard was situated at the side of the old river at the southern end of what is now Robinson Road (Mr. 'Dick' Robinson was a local sailing ship owner, a harbour pilot and latterly a member of the Urban District Council.) The shipyard was noted for its covered slipway, which enabled building to proceed in any weather. John Gray built some quite large sailing vessels here in the early part of the last century. The best known craft to come from this yard was the 'Sussex Maid'. The cottages right are in Sussex Square. This picture was taken about 1875.

61. Post-women of Newhaven during the First World War. The fair sex also infiltrated into the male dominated dockland scene with the pressure of work to get the supplies across to the Western front. Those working at the Heighton Munitions Works, showing their stamina when they formed a bucket chain to bring water from the pond to a fire at an explosives dump. They and the men who extinguished the blaze, were awarded collective medals for bravery and devotion to duty.

62. A much changed vista, from under the front garden trees of Saxonholme on 13th August 1920. The occasion is the unveiling of the Transport Memorial, which for reasons of traffic problems was moved after the Second World War to its present position at West Quay. During the First World War, Newhaven was the main supply port for the British forces at the Western Front. Numerous transports from 200 to 2,000 tons were employed in this non stop work, at times they moored three abreast all along East Quay and singly along Railway Quay and up into North Quay.

63. A Naval Volunteers funeral makes its sad way along Lewes Road to the cemetery in about 1906. The 'Lewes Road Tavern' can just be seen on the right. The prominent houses of Elphick Road and to the left 'Lee Cottages' have all gone to be replaced by the block of flats. 'Lee Court', the area around here, was known as 'The Holmes'.

64. It's thirsty work, threshing for farmer Hobbs, but the barrel poised on a bucket has provided new life for these worthies. The photograph was taken on the then unbuilt land behind the 'Sheffield Arms Hotel' and the houses are those of the coastguards, with the rear wash houses obscured by steam.

65. Langridge Bros. had a haulage business based behind the 'Railway Hotel'. It is thought that the boiler here in transit is destined for the Silica Works then on land between Robinson and Elphick Roads. At this plant beach boulders were crushed to abrasive powder. The railway police box remains, but with the 1866 swing bridge removed, the road leads nowhere.

66. Inside the west wing of the Tarpaulin factory, West Quay, about 1918. This massive corrugated structure was situated between the Bonded warehouse and the 'Ark Inn'. Sheets to cover railway waggons were made here until 1923 and repairs carried out until the 1940's. The sheets were made of stout canvas which were double boiled in linseed oil mixed with vegetable black; this was made up into a 90 gallon quantity in a large barrel kept in an outhouse. Each side of a sheet was given two coats. The numerous ropes seen at either side are for hoisting the sheets to dry, some of which can be seen hanging from the centre rear. The large bags for containing the 104 tons of concrete used in the foundations of the breakwater were also made here.

67. Early view south from the swing bridge. The single funnelled tug is believed to be the 'Victoria' which boasted a trackway between the paddle boxes, with a heavily weighted truck normally fixed amidships, when the tug was required to make a sharp turn, the truck would be pushed to one side, thus lifting the opposite paddle out of the water and with the helm hard over a small circle could be achieved.

68. 'Sheerlegs', a tripod crane 105 feet high, left, capable of lifting 80 tons, is seen with a ships boiler ready for hoisting by its steam winch. This landmark was positioned between the marine workshops and the carpenter's shop. Erected in 1881, it was felled for scrap at 5.30 a.m. 5th August 1965. The near paddle steamer is one of the twin sisters 'Normandy' or 'Brittany' (1882-1902). The vessel on the gridiron is the 'Seaford'. The picture was taken about 1895.

69. A view which always looks better at high water! South from the swing bridge about 1900. The steamers left to right are P.S. 'Paris III' with alongside the harbour pinnace 'Pinafore', beyond the hopper 'Trident' and farthest the excursion paddler 'Sussex Belle'. On the right side of the river is possibly the pleasure steamer 'Princess May' and nearest the camera the paddling tug 'Tipper'.

70. Across the East Battery at the Fort towards a new west pier lighthouse, thus suggesting the date to be in the early 1880's. The houses of Fort Rise now cover the area of the old gun emplacements.

71. The Earl of Sheffield's tramway. In 1878, agreement was reached between the Newhaven Harbour Company and the Earl of Sheffield, which allowed each to cross over the others land, the Harbour Company to reach the breakwater to be, and the Earl to convey chalk and so on to the riverside from his Meeching Quarry. There were 90 wooden trucks. The last three horses into the 1930's were Captain, Colonel and Prince. Three tons was the load. A horse linked to the first truck would walk, pulling the truck until a certain distance from the stage, then it would be coaxed into a trot. As the horse reached the harbour side, the handler would pull a cord operating a quick release and lead the horse clear of the track. The truck would trundle onto the stage. The rails at the outer extreme were dipped and bent upwards so that the leading wheels dropped and stopped dead, with the result that the container part of the truck, which was hinged at the front end, tipped up and shot the chalk into the ship's hold.

72. From Meeching Downs across an unfinished Fort Road, over Huggett's field to a unique harbour scene. The sailing vessel left, having probably brought a cargo of ice blocks from Scandinavia, although not at a chalk loading stage, may well be waiting her turn to take on ballast. This is supported by the two trains of loaded trucks near the present tug stage, where the dredger 'Hercules' is at work. The photograph was taken about 1900.

73. Before 1901, from the vicinity of First Avenue. The hedge and fencing from the right makes up Grays Lane leading past the large semi-detached houses in Hillcrest Road down to Fort Road. The field adjoining Grays Lane is now Brooks Close. Alongside the 'London and Paris Hotel' is moored one of the Caen steamers which were sold in 1901.

74. A rural scene with a marine background at about the turn of the century. The picture has been taken from the First- Second Avenue area. The large house is Grays on the site of which is now an infants-school.

75. Much excitement in Newhaven on the 26th July 1912, when the intrepid air ace Graham White, brought his frail seaplane into the harbour, during a coastal exhibition of the craft promoting his cause 'Wake up England', which wording was painted on both sides of the small fuselage of the plane. His concern for our military apathy only had two years to wait for its redemption! The mail boat, rear, is the French 'Newhaven' built the year before. Hydraulic cranes are on the East Quay.

76. During the First World War a considerable seaplane base was established on the east beach with large hangers and a complement of about 150. The planes were brought down a slipway built across the shingle, on wheels and launched much like small craft at the marina. The planes carried bombs and were used for seeking U Boats, protecting convoys and general spotting duties. Looking towards the east pier, in this picture can be seen a 'Short' 184, built by the Brush Electrical Co Ltd. of Loughborough. It was fitted with a 260 h.p. Sunbeam engine.